STICKER MOSAICS

REPTILES

APPLESAUCE
· PRESS ·

13-Digit ISBN: 978-1-64643-344-5
10-Digit ISBN: 1-64643-344-0

This book may be ordered by mail from the publisher. Please include $5.99 for postage and handling. Please support your local bookseller first!

Books published by Cider Mill Press Book Publishers are available at special discounts for bulk purchases in the United States by corporations, institutions, and other organizations. For more information, please contact the publisher.

Applesauce Press is an imprint of
Cider Mill Press Book Publishers
"Where good books are ready for press"
501 Nelson Place
Nashville, Tennessee 37214

cidermillpress.com
Typography: Josefin Sans, Industry Inc

Printed in China

23 24 25 26 27 DSC 5 4 3 2 1
First Edition

HOW TO USE THIS BOOK

CREATING YOUR OWN STICKER MOSAIC IS SIMPLE.
Peel a sticker from the corresponding sticker sheet in
the back of the book. You can tear the art pages or
sticker sheets out of the book so you don't have to flip
back and forth. You will see that each sticker has a
number. All you have to do is match the number on the
sticker to the number on the silhouette. Once placed,
the stickers aren't removable, so put them down
carefully. Watch as your reptile puzzles come to life
in full color, sticker by sticker!

CONTENTS

7. Philippine Sailfin Lizard

8. Eastern Diamondback Rattlesnake

9. American Crocodile

10. Giant Tortoise

11. Frilled Lizard

12. Yellow-Bellied Sea Snake

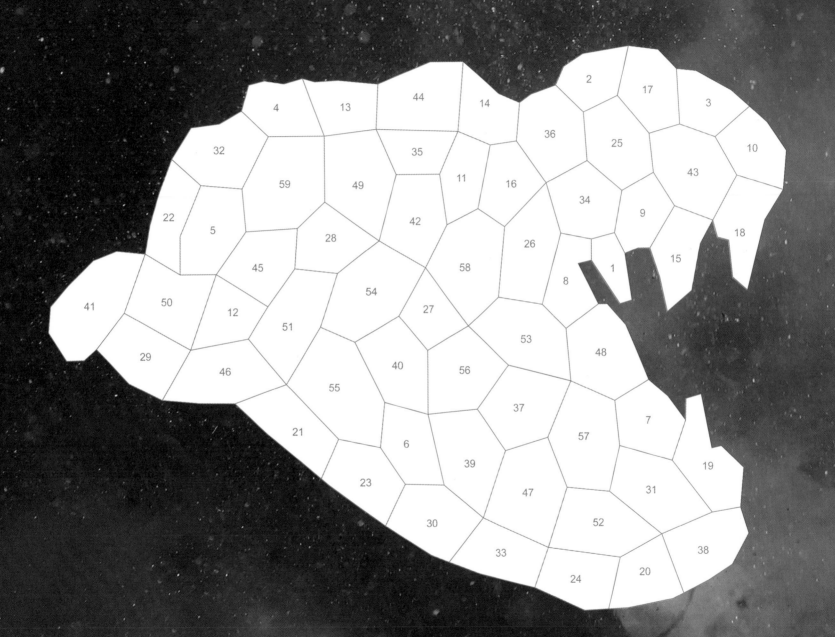

Saltwater Crocodile
Crocodylus porosus

Where: Australia, New Guinea, and Indonesia

Size: Males 17 to 20 feet (5 to 6 meters); female 8 to 9 feet (2.43 to 2.75 meters)

Physical Profile: A massive crocodile with scales, visible teeth, and large, clawed feet.

Christmas Marine Iguana
Amblyrhynchus cristatus venustissimus

Where: Galápagos Islands

Size: Males 4 to 5 feet (1.2 to 1.5 meters); females 2 to 3 feet (0.6 to 0.9 meter)

Physical Profile: A bright red and green iguana with a thickset body, short limbs, and a row of spines from neck to tail.

Hawksbill Sea Turtle
Eretmochelys imbricata

Where: Atlantic Ocean, Indian Ocean, and Pacific Ocean

Size: 2 to 3 feet (0.6 to 0.9 meter)

Physical Profile: A sea turtle with a sharp, curved beak and overlapping scutes that give its shell a saw-like appearance.

Giant Girdled Lizard
Smaug giganteus

Where: South Africa
Size: 1 to 1.5 feet (0.3 to 0.45 meter)
Physical Profile: A lizard with pointed, spiny scales that act as armor.

Philippine Pit Viper
Trimeresurus flavomaculatus

Where: Philippines

Size: 1 to 1.5 feet (0.3 to 0.45 meter)

Physical Profile: A green viper with reddish-brown markings and pit organs on its face that allow it to sense heat.

Thorny Devil
Moloch horridus

Where: Australia

Size: 6 to 8 inches (15 to 20 centimeters)

Physical Profile: A small lizard with spotty coloring and large spines all over its textured body.

Philippine Sailfin Lizard
Hydrosaurus pustulatus

Where: Philippines

Size: 2 to 3 feet (0.6 to 0.9 meter)

Physical Profile: A lizard with flattened toes and a 2- to 3-inch sail on its back.

12
11
70
58
39
33
37
10
5
49
32
27
38
6
13
9
31
1
7
64
71
63
26
34
14
48
20
57
42
4
50
62
25
36
15
8
30
41
56
2
3
65
51
29
24
54
35
19
16
55
17
59
66
68
52
23
61
21
40
60
18
53
28
45
67
43
22
47
46
44
69

Eastern Diamondback Rattlesnake
Crotalus adamanteus

Where: Southeastern United States

Size: 4 to 6 feet (1.2 to 1.8 meters)

Physical Profile: A large, venomous viper with a rattle-like tail tip and yellow or tan scales in a diamond pattern along its body.

American Crocodile
Crocodylus acutus

Where: Southern North America, Central America, and South America

Size: Males 20 feet (6.1 meters); females 12 feet (3.65 meters)

Physical Profile: A crocodile with grayish coloring, an elongated snout, strong jaws, and a long, powerful tail.

Giant Tortoise
Chelonoidis duncanensis

Where: Galápagos Islands

Size: 4 to 5 feet (1.2 to 1.5 meters)

Physical Profile: A massive, brownish-gray tortoise with a thick, protective shell.

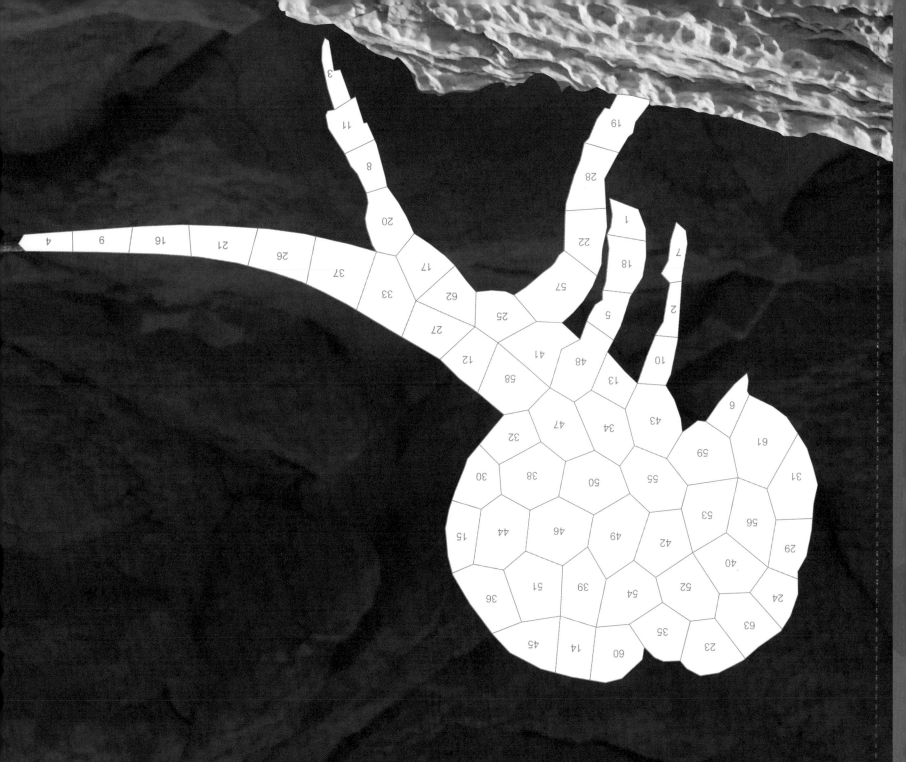

Frilled Lizard
Chlamydosaurus kingii

Where: Australia and New Guinea

Size: 3 feet (0.9 meter)

Physical Profile: A lizard with a pleated flap of skin around its neck that expands to make its body look bigger.

Yellow-Bellied Sea Snake
Hydrophis platurus

Where: Indian Ocean and Pacific Ocean

Size: 3 to 4 feet (0.9 to 1.2 meters)

Physical Profile: A saltwater snake with a vibrant yellow stripe along the underside of its body.

STICKERS

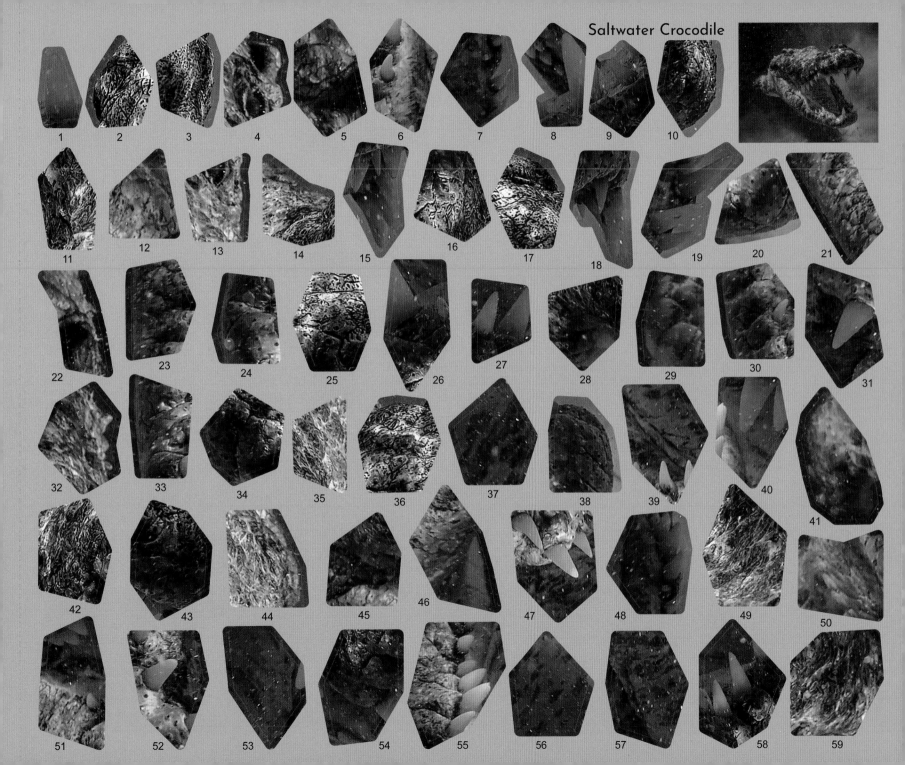

Saltwater Crocodile

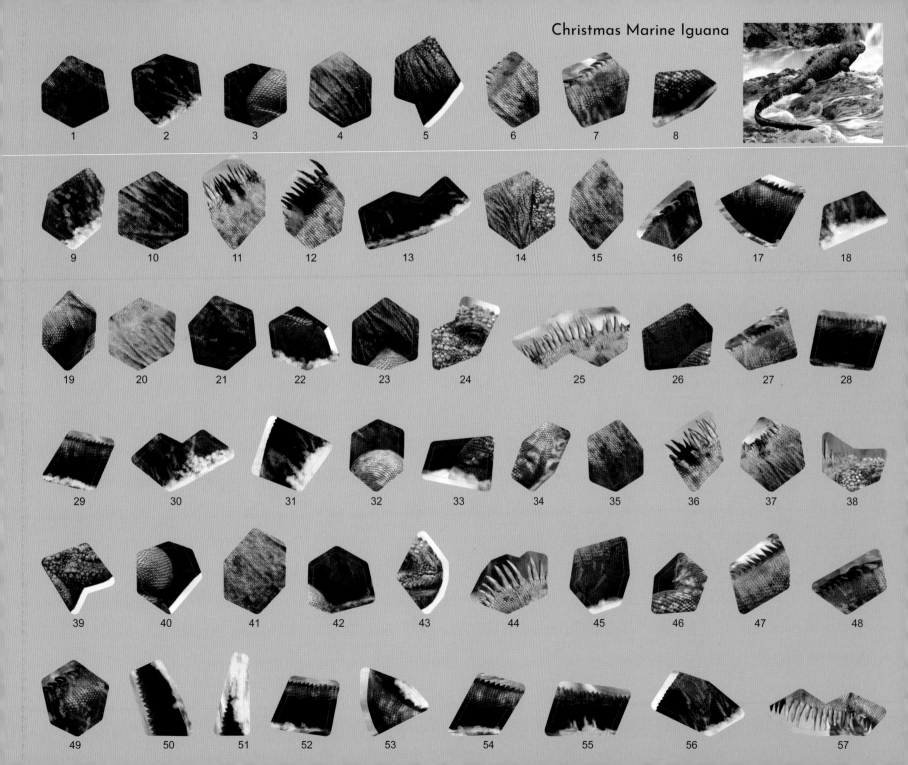

Christmas Marine Iguana

Hawksbill Sea Turtle

Giant Girdled Lizard

Philippine Pit Viper

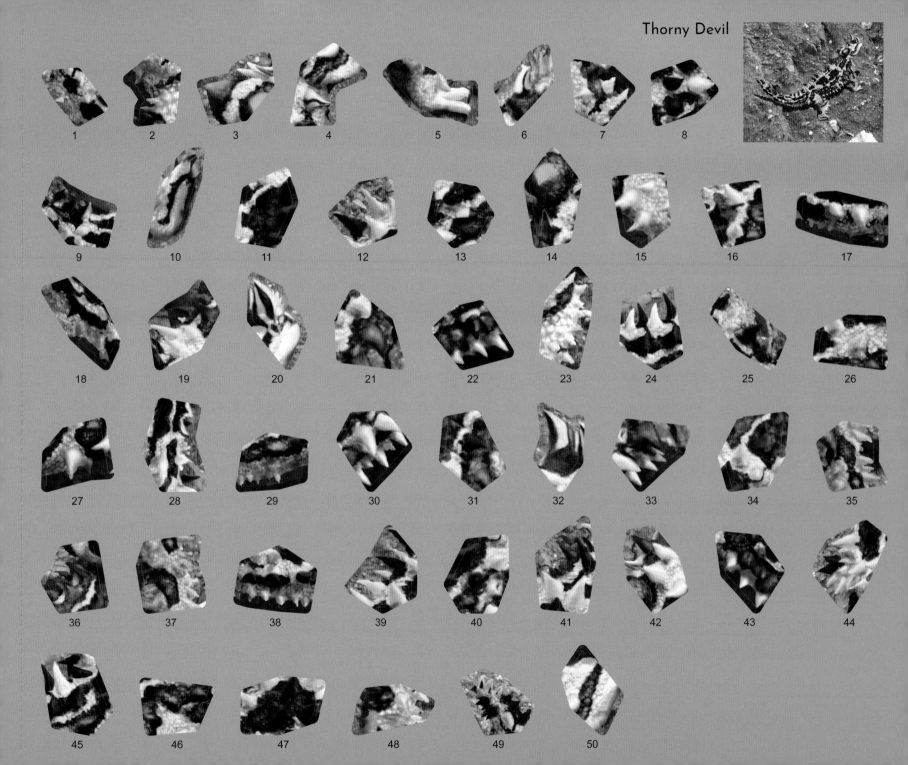

Thorny Devil

American Crocodile

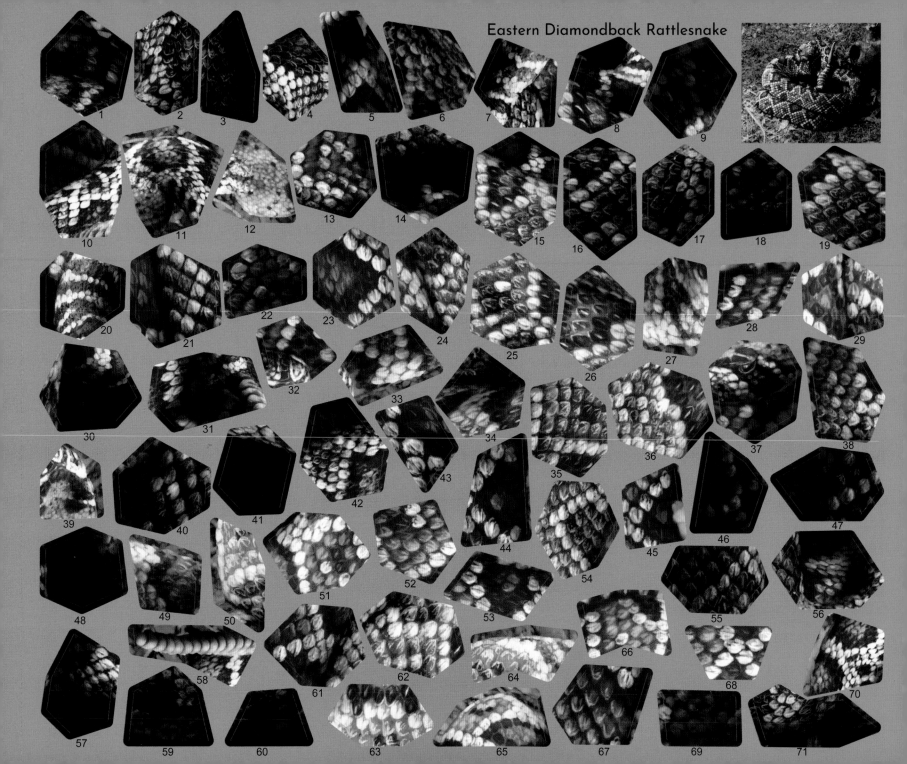

Eastern Diamondback Rattlesnake

Philippine Sailfin Lizard

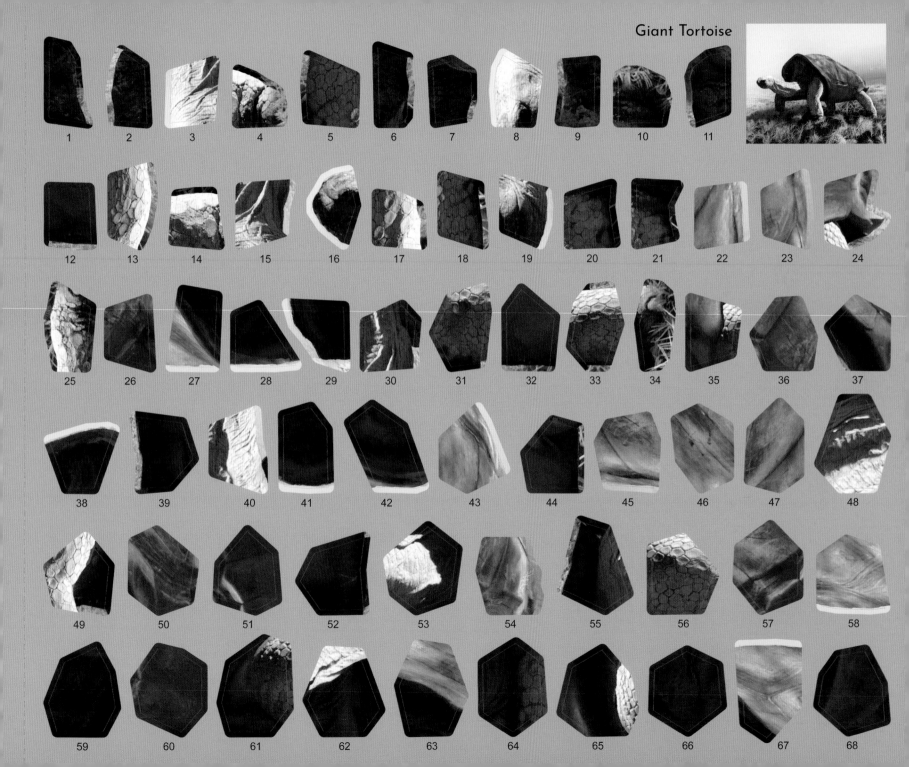

Giant Tortoise

Frilled Lizard

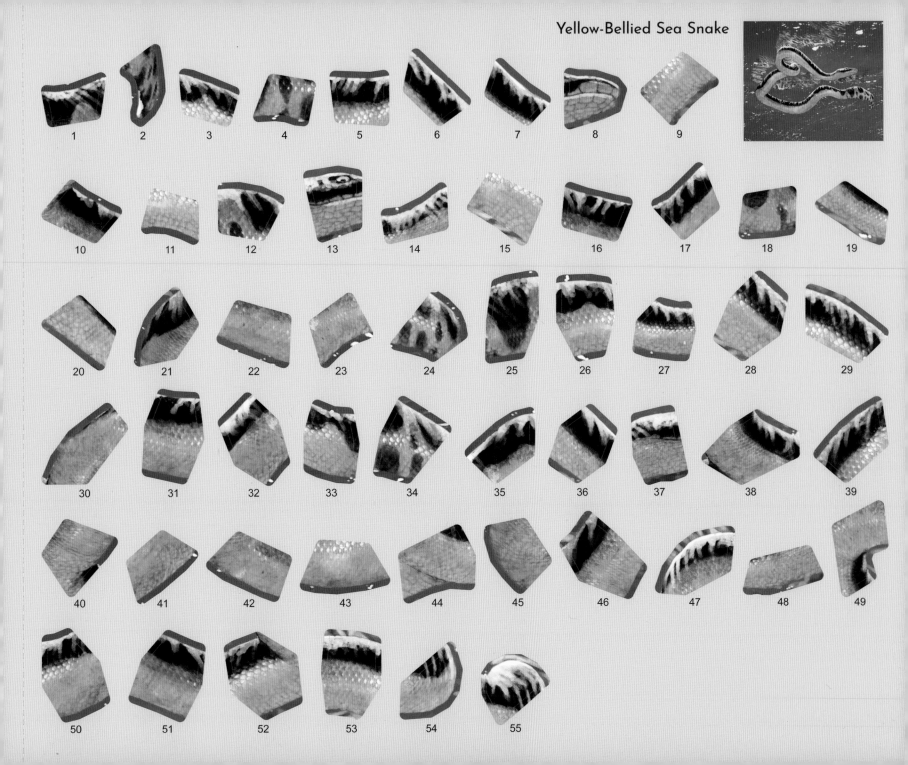

Yellow-Bellied Sea Snake

1   2   3   4   5   6   7   8   9

10   11   12   13   14   15   16   17   18   19

20   21   22   23   24   25   26   27   28   29

30   31   32   33   34   35   36   37   38   39

40   41   42   43   44   45   46   47   48   49

50   51   52   53   54   55

ABOUT APPLESAUCE PRESS

Good ideas ripen with time. From seed to harvest, Applesauce Press crafts books with beautiful designs, creative formats, and kid-friendly information on a variety of fascinating topics. Like our parent company, Cider Mill Press Book Publishers, our press bears fruit twice a year, publishing a new crop of titles each spring and fall.

"Where good books are ready for press"
501 Nelson Place
Nashville, Tennessee 37214

cidermillpress.com